LIGHT
FOR THE
PATH

LIGHT
FOR THE
PATH

Six Steps for Effective
Scripture Memorization

Marla Kohmetscher

ILLUMIFY
MEDIA.COM

LIGHT FOR THE PATH

Copyright © 2026 by Marla Kohmetscher

Unless otherwise noted, all Scripture is taken from NIV 1984 Holy Bible, New International Version®, NIV® Copyright ©1973, 1978, 1984 by Biblica, Inc.® Used by permission. All rights reserved worldwide.

The views and opinions expressed in this book are those of the author and do not necessarily reflect the official policy or position of Illumify Media Global.

Published by
Illumify Media Global
www.IllumifyMedia.com
"Let's bring your book to life!"

Paperback ISBN: 978-1-964251-96-7

Typeset by Art Innovations (http://artinnovations.in/)
Cover design by Debbie Lewis

Printed in the United States of America

CONTENTS

INTRODUCTION

*A*udrey heard the familiar ding and glanced at the incoming text from her friend Lori. *My heart is broken. Wade just handed me divorce papers.*

I'm so sorry! You want me to come over? Audrey texted back.

Lori replied, *YES.* Audrey hopped in her car but began to panic on the way there. She rehearsed the words she could say, but everything sounded hollow. She wanted to help but feared doing more harm to her friend's heart.

When she arrived, she gave Lori an extended hug, and they moved to the kitchen table where they often sat for coffee. Audrey listened as Lori shared details of the devastating conversation she had had with her husband that morning. When it came time for her to speak, she knew she should say something spiritual. After all, they were both Christians. Their families had gone to the same church for years. As her mind searched for solid answers, however, platitudes came out instead.

"You've been living like this for so long. Maybe it's a blessing in disguise."

After a few more tortured minutes of talking, Audrey asked if there was another woman. When Lori stated there wasn't, Audrey said, "At least he isn't cheating. It could be worse."

For some reason, her friend started crying again. After a while the tears subsided, and Audrey suddenly felt irritated. "Just let him leave. You deserve better!" she said.

Lori sighed deeply. "I need to rest now. I'll call you later."

As Audrey prepared to leave, she hugged her friend again. "I will pray for you," she said. "And you might want to call Pastor Scott. He'll be able to help you with this." She waved as she left. "Let me know if you need anything."

Hopefully, we wouldn't be this ineffective at loving our friends when they go through difficult times. However, we've all experienced off-hand comments, unhelpful platitudes, and Scripture used out of context. It's hard enough to be vulnerable, but when we share our pain and someone makes it worse, we often stop talking altogether.

A Better Way

Wouldn't it be nice to know what to say and what to avoid saying? As Christians, we want to empathize, encourage, and gently speak the truth to each other. We can accomplish this best when we have an intimate relationship with Christ. The more we know His heart, the better our message to someone like Lori would be.

We get to know God's heart by spending time in His Word and renewing our minds with truth. In addition, the more Scripture we hide in our hearts, the easier it is for the Holy Spirit to bring those verses to mind when we need them—both for ourselves and others.

> *"A word aptly spoken is like apples of gold in settings of silver."*
> *~ Proverbs 25:11*

What's your history concerning Scripture memory? Can you relate to any of these statements? Underline all that apply.

- It's a struggle.
- I don't have the time.
- I haven't tried.
- I'm too old to start now.
- I remember some verses from childhood.
- I don't have a good system.
- I have trouble retaining memory verses.
- I'm new in my faith.
- I struggle to use Scripture in my daily life.

No matter what your story is, once you've gone through this study, you will have the tools necessary to memorize more verses and even longer passages of Scripture. Most important, you will learn to incorporate Scripture memory into your daily life, letting the Holy Spirit move verses from your head to your heart and speak truth over circumstances you face in your life. You will also be a more effective friend.

My Story

Growing up in a church with a Bible memory program, I learned many passages of Scripture as a young child. The goal of the program was to recite verses and their references without error. Once confident that a passage was memorized, I approached an adult after church and asked if I could recite my memory verse. If the person agreed, I would hand over my Bible and attempt to recite the passage and reference without any mistakes. If I missed even one word, I would be given another chance. If I failed that attempt, I would have to wait until the following Sunday to get it right.

This program came with rewards—mainly books, which caused me extreme happiness. Besides the benefits of prizes, learning to interact with adults and developing creative ways of retaining Scripture was beneficial. As time went on, the verses got longer, and I struggled to memorize them. Yet, with a lot of repetition, I was able to memorize beautiful passages of Scripture as a child. At that time, however, the connection between God's Word and my everyday life was missing. My childhood view of God didn't progress past the milk stage for quite a while. After several years (and a million messes and mistakes), I pleaded with Jesus to come back into my life . . . and soon realized He never left. I was the one who had walked away.

God set my life on a brand-new path. Many of the verses I memorized as a child came back to me, and they meant something now! Passages penetrated my heart, changed my thoughts, and then my life. My faith was growing, and I started to understand the benefits and blessings of hiding God's Word in my heart.

Little Scripture cards were scattered around my house. They were my lifeline to the truth I desperately needed. As the years went by, I joined an intensive Bible memory program. After getting my certificate, I realized the verses were too many to hold in my heart. Some of the Scripture faded in my mind and weren't being used effectively. Although that time was beneficial, it was a struggle to put the Scriptures into practice.

Before long, a ministry opportunity arose, and I spent a decade as director of a crisis pregnancy center (CPC). Having been a devastated sixteen-year-old with an unplanned pregnancy, I knew the hard choices these young women would have to make. As for me, after weeks of tearful discussions, I made the difficult decision to keep my child and become a seventeen-year-old mom with my parents' help.

My time at the CPC was filled with loving, caring for, and encouraging young women during a difficult time of their lives, along with over forty believers from all backgrounds, various churches, and communities. We also spoke at schools and events about abstinence and ministered to those who chose abortion and provided a way for them to process their pain and receive forgiveness and restoration.

Later, my husband got a new job in another city, and we moved there after a difficult season in our lives. Our children were raised and gone. Soon, our marriage was gone too: a divorce I emphatically didn't want. After spending an extended time alone and immersing myself in God's Word, the Lord met me in a miraculous way. He reached into the worst of situations and brought about good. I learned firsthand about how He comforts the brokenhearted and renews those who are crushed in spirit.

After a while, I decided to attend college and several years later ended up with a bachelor's degree in Christian ministry and a minor in biblical studies. Over twenty years later, here I am, recently retired from ministry as a chaplain at a faith-based hospital where people experience some of the darkest, deepest pain imaginable. This is where God's Word also came alive, not necessarily in verses that I quoted to patients—but the truths found in Scripture. I shared from my firsthand knowledge of what I knew of God's love, mercy, grace, forgiveness, healing and peace.

As you learn and internalize Scripture, ask God to use it mightily in your life for your every need, no matter who you are or what you've gone through. And I pray He will use what you memorize to minister to others.

The Bible was not given to us to increase our knowledge; it was given
to us to change our lives.
~ D.L. Moody

Where We Are Headed

We'll start off by discussing which Scriptures to memorize. The Bible is full of verses, but which ones are most important to commit to memory? We want to memorize those verses with the greatest impact for our personal lives and those that are vital to share with others. This is unique for everyone, so prayerfully consider what God wants you to learn at this point in your walk with the Lord.

As you make your way through Scripture, it's important to understand the context and determine how—or if—it applies to you. Some verses in the Word are descriptive, while others are prescriptive. Is this Scripture something to obey, a promise to cherish, or is it meant for another time, place, or person?

Another important aspect of memorization is the various techniques used to learn different types of Scripture. I will share a few, but in time, you will develop those techniques that work best for you or may even discover others along the way.

It's important to become familiar with resources to help you understand God's Word as a whole. Utilize online tools as well as printed resources. Sometimes we don't understand context, concepts, words or history—and it's best to look up those things we question.

Next, I will provide information on how to create a personalized index card notebook. I've found it helpful to have my verses available all in one place; so, I've purchased 3 X 5 index card notebooks to keep them in. Each one holds fifty verses.

As you embark on this journey, you may choose to go it alone. However, there is much to be said about accountability. Do you know someone else who wants to memorize Scripture? Maybe a friend, your spouse, or a women's group at church? The Lord states clearly that we are to encourage one another. This study would be a great way to do that!

The Six Rs, a method I designed to facilitate memorization, will be helpful during this study and most importantly, after. My prayer is that you will learn to love hiding God's Word in your heart and continue doing so throughout your life.

In part 2 of this study, I've chosen three verses from three different books of the Bible:

1. A morning verse from Psalms,
2. A noon verse from Proverbs, and
3. A night verse from Philippians.

This will help us meditate on God's Word throughout the day. I chose to emphasis the use of Scripture, not the number of verses to memorize. My hope is that this study gives you a good foundation to memorize more on your own or with others.

The New International Version is the Bible I use for this study. I encourage you to use it for this time. I was in a Bible memory group once where we used three different versions. As we recited our verses out loud, we often messed up when our turn came to quote our verse. Whatever Bible version you want to use after this study is up to you. However, it will make things easier if you use the same version as everyone else if you are in a group.

Part 2 includes three weeks of memorizing the morning, noon, and night verses. I will introduce the books, providing some context so you can better understand and use God's Word correctly. You may already be familiar with these three books, but not everyone is, so tag along. Perhaps you'll discover new insights. God's Word has a way of doing that!

Throughout the study, there will be exercises to help us meditate on the meaning of the passage, while also considering various ways to memorize. Before we get too far, we will take a creative break. You will need to purchase a spiral index card notebook to keep track of your verses plus have room for many more after this study is done.

In addition, I will give you a few scenarios to help you think through the truths of Scripture and how to use God's Word effectively in your life, and when you are called to be there for others.

"All Scripture is God-breathed and is useful for teaching, rebuking, correcting, and training in righteousness, so that the servant of God may be thoroughly equipped for every good work."
2 Timothy 3:16–17

Lord,

We praise You for Your precious Word that overflows with promises and precepts to help us in our spiritual growth. We desire to absorb what You have for us and live it out in our daily lives. Clear out any confusion, discouragement, or fear of failure. Since we know it's Your desire for us to hide Your Word in our hearts, we entrust our minds and hearts to You in pursuit of this discipline. Guide us ever closer to You, and may we encourage each other along the way. In Your precious Son's name, amen.

PART ONE

WEEK 1

WHAT TO MEMORIZE

"When an old minister was asked to give his favorite verse, he replied, 'When I think of a favorite verse, half a dozen come to my mind. On stormy days I want a cloak; cold days I want the sunny side of the wall; hot days I want a shady path; now I want a shower of manna; now I want a drink of cool living water; now I want a sword. I might as well try to tell you which is my favorite eye. The one I might love is the one I might soon need and want.'"

~ Anonymous

Have you already memorized Scripture, don't know how, or have tried and failed too often? Most of us fall somewhere in between: we want more of God's Word internalized but feel discouraged by our lack of progress or abilities. While we could strive in this study to commit long passages to memory and possibly succeed with one or two, it's more important to start small and build necessary skills. What matters most is not where we end up, such as knowing one hundred verses by heart, but that our desire to know and love God grows, and that we learn to listen to the voice of the Holy Spirit. It's only then that we can use His Word effectively.

Handling God's Word

The Bible contains sixty-six books: thirty-nine in the Old Testament and twenty-seven in the New Testament, with various genres from many different authors. These books contain history, prophecy, poetry, songs, stories, sayings, parables, prayers, letters, and more—all inspired by the Holy Spirit. We could spend every minute of our lives immersed in its pages and still not understand the depth of God's love for us.

An old hymn's third stanza says it best, I think:

Could we with ink the ocean fill
And were the skies of parchment made;
Were every stalk on earth a quill
And every man a scribe by trade;
To write the love of God above
Would drain the ocean dry;
Nor could the scroll contain the whole,
Though stretched from sky to sky.

Refrain:
Oh, love of God,
how rich and pure!
How measureless and strong!
It shall forever more endure—
The saints' and angels' song.[1]

Fredrick Lehman wrote the refrain and two of the three stanzas of the well-known hymn "The Love of God" in 1917. This third stanza, however, is anonymous: said to be found penciled on a wall in an insane asylum—reminding us that God can speak to us anywhere.

---

1   Nazarene Publishing House, Songs that are Different, 1924.

It's important to handle God's Word with care. We don't want to misrepresent God or manipulate His Word to say something untrue or misleading. The Bible is readily available to us, and it's a privilege that many in the world can't fathom let alone enjoy.

When we haphazardly pluck verses from the Bible, it may seem harmless, but it can be detrimental, taking us down paths that are hard to return from. We can also lead others in the wrong direction by our lack of spiritual discernment. Not everything in Scripture is literal or meant for us. If we're not careful, we can bend the Word to say something we *want* to hear instead of the truth.

The best way to explore and choose verses to memorize is to study them in context. Do you have to reach far to make it mean something? Does the verse cause you to question something you've been taught? Do more mature Christians have a problem with something you believe? Does anyone challenge your view?

God's Word is vast, and its treasures are endless. A person could read, study, meditate, memorize, and mine every nugget of Scripture gold they could, but it would only be a start. No one has ever mastered God's Word, though many have tried.

Hermeneutics

Hermeneutics is the branch of knowledge that deals with interpretation. It is how we assess Scripture accurately. According to the book *Grasping God's Word* by J. Scott Duvall and John Daniel Hays it's important to embark on an interpretive journey when reading and applying Scripture. "We are separated from the biblical audience by culture and customs, language, situation, and a vast expanse of time." This journey involves looking into the past context, discovering the differences and noting the similarities of both then and now; it involves bridging the gap—and finding principles for our lives today.

To delve into this topic thoroughly would take the rest of this study, so I will just wade into the shallow part of its vast ocean of thought. (Truthfully, I'm still learning to be a good swimmer in this sea.) However, I'm acutely aware that using Scripture out of context is how people can get off track, or cults can start; many people have been sidetracked by false teaching. Always ask *who, what, where, when, and why.* Don't make a Scripture verse mean more than it does.

In order to not go out on a limb, it's important to have access to a Bible dictionary, commentaries, and various authors' insights on Scripture. These days it's simple to locate information. Most commentaries and Bible dictionaries are accessible online—such as www.biblestudytools.com or www.biblegateway.com. Find out what trustworthy pastors, authors, and commentators have to say about passages of Scripture you want to memorize.

In addition, the more we study the Bible as a whole, the more precious and personal God's Word becomes. The immeasurable value of this Book lays out God's deep love for each one of us: His free gift of salvation for those who place their faith in Christ.

> *"For God so loved the world that he gave his one and only Son, that*
> *whoever believes in him shall not perish*
> *but have eternal life."*
> ~ John 3:16

Memorize What Matters

God's Word is important for every aspect of our lives. We often try to discern answers to questions or decide what to do in various situations. However, when we have verses stored in our mind and heart, it's much easier for the Holy Spirit to speak to us: infinitely better than a frantic search through the Word, opening random pages in desperate need of help.

How do we find relevant verses to learn by heart? Consider these questions when choosing Scriptures:

- Does this verse help me think right thoughts?
- Could this Scripture keep me from sin?
- Could I use this passage to encourage other believers?
- How could this verse calm my fears?

- Can I speak with an unbeliever using this precept?
- Will this draw me closer to Christ?
- Does this passage cause me to worship God?
- Could I personalize this section of Scripture for a prayer?
- Is this verse important to remember when I'm discouraged?
- Could I use this verse to assure someone about their position in Christ?
- Would I be able to lead someone to the Lord with Scripture?

Many verses come our way when we read God's Word, spend extended time with Him, listen to sermons, attend Bible studies, seminars, or by time spent with other believers. Passages of Scripture can be formed into prayers, used in worship, or put on for armor. When you encounter a verse that God speaks to you about, write it down, along with a date or the occasion when it came to your attention. Some people don't like to highlight, underline, or write in their Bibles. I'm not one of those people. If you feel differently, that's okay. Use a journal to record what God is showing you. Jot down how verses on these subjects could help you.

Father,

We are in awe of You. We praise you for giving us your Holy Word. May we use it effectively; may it help us with life here on earth and equip us for eternity with You. Help us dive into its riches, learning, growing, and finding ways to express our love. We long to use Your Words correctly. Steer us away from anything that is not the truth or misrepresents Your majesty. Place verses in front of us that You want us to know, verses to meditate on and memorize to use for Your glory. In Christ's name, amen.

HOW TO MEMORIZE SCRIPTURE

"Remember Whose you are and Whom you serve. Provoke yourself to recollection, and your affection for God will increase tenfold; your imagination will not be starved any longer, but will be quick and enthusiastic, and your hope will be inexpressibly bright."

~ Oswald Chambers

Abundant ways exist to help facilitate Scripture memory. If one method doesn't work, you can always try another. God made you unique in the way you learn, so don't give up. In time you will find that you will develop your own methods. Pray often about what you meditate on and memorize. After all, this discipline is something God desires for you. He will help you accomplish it.

Mnemonics

Mnemonics plays a significant role in helping us remember important information. We learned various methods in elementary school under this banner. We sang the ABCs, rehearsed rhymes, broke big words apart to spell them correctly, learned grammar rules, acronyms, play on words, history facts, geography, and more with this method.

According to medical social worker Esther Heerema, there are ten main ways mnemonics can be helpful: Keyword, Chunking, Musical, Acronyms, Acrostics,

Rhymes, Making Connections, Method of Loci, Peg Method, and Linking (or Chaining) System. Looking these systems up as you continue to memorize will be beneficial.

Make a Joyful Noise

Songs, hymns and choruses are often taken from Scripture. Consequently, if you sing along with Christian music in your car, in church, or at a concert, you might learn verses without trying.

Here are a few choruses that come to mind:

The name of the Lord is a strong tower. The righteous run into it and they are safe. (Proverbs 18:10)

Great is Thy faithfulness, (Lamentations 3:23–24)

This is the day that the Lord has made. We will rejoice and be glad in it (Psalm 118:24)

I will sing of the mercies of the Lord forever... (Psalm 89:1)

Psalms are full of songs you most likely know. Spend some time in this book and you will find them. David's time on earth, both as a shepherd and a king, gave us many of the most beautiful words ever written.

In addition, we run across other contemporary choruses as we read God's Word. Keep an eye out for lyrics you can learn.

Accountability

Memorization can be accomplished alone. However, when you learn alongside others, you receive encouragement and accountability, which is always beneficial. Hebrews 10:24 says "And let us consider how we may spur one another on toward love and good deeds." Prayerfully consider how God wants you to proceed after this study. Will you incorporate memorization into your quiet time? Would you prefer to pursue it alone at your own pace? Will you learn scripture with a group of believers, or partner with your spouse or a friend? Spend some time and pray about it. Whatever way you choose, make sure it's a good fit for you.

Write Your Verses in One Place

A place dedicated to Scripture you memorize will help when you review them all in one sitting (which you will want to do often!). That's why I recommend you get a 3 x 5 spiral index card notebook where you can keep all your verses. As you flip through this special little book you will find it much easier to review than if you had random notes and scattered verses lying around.

A great way to start your memorization journey is to personalize your index card notebook. It's fun to do this in a group setting where there are plenty of materials, ideas, and creativity floating around. If you need inspiration when you make your notebook, it's okay to look over someone's shoulder. If you choose to do this study alone, please take the time to make a personal index notebook.

Basic Materials Needed:
Index card spiral notebook
White cardstock
Glue stick
Clear transfer paper
A pair of scissors
Old magazines

My favorite medium when creating scripture notebooks is collage. Yours might be something else. Whatever it is, gather those supplies and make it meaningful to you.

Three Examples

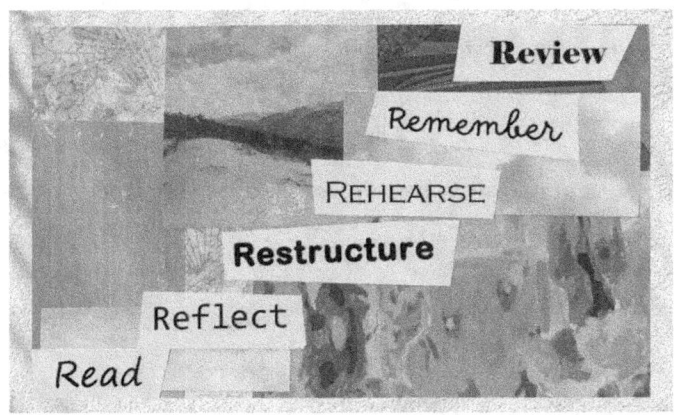

Lord,

Strengthen us for the days ahead, to meet challenges with Your empowerment. We long to know You more and have sweeter fellowship with You. We ask You to meet us right where we are and help us grow in ways that you have designed for us. Sharpen our minds and pierce our hearts with Your Word. In Jesus's precious name, Amen.

WEEK 3

SKILLS TO MASTER

"God's strength behind you, His concern for you, His love within you, and His arms beneath you are more than sufficient for the job ahead of you."

~William Arthur Ward

After several stops and starts, I created a specific way to help with Scripture memory. The words are in the form of alliteration, each beginning with the letter *R.* I encourage you to memorize these six words for future use and write them in the front of your index notebook.

READ
REFLECT
RESTRUCTURE
REHEARSE
REMEMBER
REVIEW

The Six Rs

READ

For each verse or passage, read it in context, surrounded by verses before and after. You may end up reading the whole chapter or book where it is found, but the goal is to know who, when, what, where, and why it was written. Look up a commentary or two on the passage to see what they say. Also, you want to determine what type of genre it is: It could be poetry, prose, song, psalm, command, prophecy, part of a letter, or a prayer. Is it applicable for today? Does it describe something or is it something God wants you to obey? Is the verse a precious promise for every believer? A warning for non-believers? An attribute of God? An Old Testament regulation?

REFLECT

How is this verse relevant in my life? Spend time contemplating the verse or verses, asking the Holy Spirit to speak truth to your heart. God may have already brought this passage to your mind in another way, and you know you'd benefit by remembering it or living it out. A good way to reflect is to talk honestly with the Lord about the verse, asking Him for insight on how to apply it to situations you regularly face. It's helpful to have a dedicated journal to record your thoughts on verses you're learning.

RESTRUCTURE

Underline, highlight, or shade the verse in your Bible. Perhaps write in the margin a date or occasion you realized you needed it. I write down Scriptures I'm learning in a my journal as well, using different fonts and styles and breaking up the lines in a way that's easier to focus on. I may even draw a simple picture, look at repeated words, think about the cadence, see words with the same starting letter, and notice forms of punctuation. After the verse is disassembled, make decisions on how you want to learn it. Keep mnemonics in mind, using them as a tool to help facilitate memorization.

REHEARSE

When you're learning a new verse, take it with you wherever you go. Repeat it often: out loud or to yourself. Practice it without looking. You might use it as a screensaver, put it on your bathroom mirror, or on a sticky note at work. Whatever the method, make sure it's at the forefront of your mind for a while. Not only will you do this with one verse, but the others you've learned need to be repeated to retain them. Since we can be certain that God's desire for us is to hide His Word in our hearts, He will help us achieve it.

REMEMBER

After you've kept a passage of Scripture close to you, you'll find it stuck in your head—which is a good place to start—but you also want it stuck in your heart. Begin to rely on the verse when you face various circumstances. The Holy Spirit will remind you of Scriptures, but only if they're already in your mind. For instance, I struggled significantly with fear and anxiety at one point in my life. A verse I memorized still helps me when I face fear today: "When I am afraid, I will trust in you. In God, whose word I praise—in God I will trust and not be afraid. What can mere mortals do to me?" (Psalm 56:3–4).

REVIEW

To retain the verses you learn, periodically review *all* of them. Set aside time to read and reflect on each one of them, perhaps recalling where, when, or how they've been helpful in your daily life. The longer your list of verses, the more time you will need to spend on this. But it's precious to meditate on how God is using His Word in your life. You will be filled with gratitude! In addition, do the following when you have shorter periods of time: repeat a verse you know, then using a word in that verse, say another verse with that word. Keep going until you can't think of another verse. This helps strengthen connections in your mind and helps with recall.

These six steps can be repeated for every verse or passage you want to memorize. Learn to enjoy the verses you have stored in your heart. We tend to think about the things we enjoy. I enjoy my grandchildren, my flower garden, sewing, photography, putting jigsaw puzzles together, and playing games. I love spending time with people I love. How much do we enjoy spending time with Jesus? As believers, it's a good question to ask ourselves.

"Let the Word of Christ dwell in you richly as you teach and admonish
one another with all wisdom, and as you sing psalms, hymns, and
spiritual songs with gratitude in your hearts to God."
~ Colossians 3:16

Thank You for providing us with the truth. So much of what we hear is skewed and warped by so many different voices. We praise Your enduring Word that never fails. Help us as we start on this memorization quest, to dig deep into Your Word, learning what we need in order to draw closer to You and be an encouragement to those around us. In Jesus's name, amen.

PART TWO

MORNING VERSE

"Nobody can take away from you those texts from the Bible which you have learned by heart."

~ Corrie ten Boom

PSALM 25:4–5

Show me your ways, O Lord, teach me your paths.
Guide me in your truth and teach me, for you are
God my Savior, and my hope is in you all day long.

When we open our Bibles down the middle, we usually land somewhere in Psalms. This book has 150 psalms of varying lengths. Psalm 117 is the shortest with just two verses, while Psalm 119 has 176 verses. Its pages have been well loved and used throughout the years, and its words echo across generations.

King David wrote most psalms, and they cover a variety of subjects and genres. As we flip through the book, we come across songs, prayers, complaints, blessings, prophecies, celebrations, laments, rebukes, and meditations.

David wasn't the only author of psalms. Also putting pen to papyrus were Solomon, Aleph, Asaph, Korah, Hermann the Ezrahite, and Moses. One of the authors just has the title Afflicted Man.

I wonder what sound the Israelites made when they stood thousands deep, worshipping God with these songs. I'm sure they also sang them in their homes, to their children, and as they went about their work. What were the melodies of Psalm 1, 24, 26, or 59? Maybe we will hear them loud and clear in heaven.

Whenever I read the Psalms, I often come across hymns we sing in church or music from contemporary artists. I hear choruses taken directly from Scripture. These Psalms are sung and recited by both Christians and Jews. As believers in Christ, under the new covenant, we know many of them are prophetic, pointing us directly to Jesus.

As we make our way through the Psalms, some passages seem harsh. They remind us that not every word is meant for personal application. We feel uncomfortable when we say parts of these psalms out loud. When I run across perplexing verses regarding vengeance on enemies, I most often substitute Satan for the enemy (because that is who he is). Always keep in mind that we live under the new covenant. Not everything is meant for us, although *all* Scripture is profitable for us (see Romans 15:4).

Place an X in the boxes when you've completed the Rs.

☐ READ

Start by reading *all* of Psalm 25 out loud. Read through it again and write down what you observe. What stands out to you?

_____

_____

_____

_____

_____

_____

_____

PSALM 25:4–5

Show me your ways, O LORD, teach me your paths.
Guide me in your truth and teach me, for you are
God my Savior, and my hope is in you all day long.

☐ REFLECT

Contemplate the meaning of these verses and how they apply to you. Can you see yourself using these verses in your life? Would it help to wake up each morning, asking God to teach you and guide you throughout the day? What will you learn about Him today, and how could the Holy Spirit use these words you memorize in times of need?

Write down your thoughts:

_____

_____

_____

_____

_____

_____

☐ RESTRUCTURE

Observe the verbs in these verses. Notice the repetition: show me, teach me, guide me, teach me. We also see that the first part is a petition, and the second part is a praise. Say these verses out loud a few times, emphasizing different words. When you're ready to memorize Psalm 25:3–4 write it in a few different fonts, examine it, take it apart, and come up with how you will learn it.

PSALM 25:4–5

Show me your ways, O Lord, teach me your paths;
guide me in your truth and teach me, for you are
God my Savior, and my hope is in you all day long.

1. _____

_____

_____

2. _____

_____

_____

3. _____

_____

_____

When you finish, write the verses in your small notebook. Also, put them other places around your home. Take a couple of notecards with you as you go about your day.

☐ REHEARSE

Read, glance at the verses, and practice them throughout the week. Keep them with you and focus on them for a few minutes. Say them in your head without looking. Visualize your walk with the Lord and let Him teach and guide you throughout the day. Talk to Him about what the passage means to you. Say the verses as a prayer.

☐ REMEMBER

Continue to repeat the verses, reflect on what they mean, and practice them until perfect. Close your Scripture notebook and say the verses without looking; if possible, hand the verses to someone and repeat them, both verses and reference.

☐ REVIEW

When you think you have mastered these verses, don't keep them tucked away. Bring them to mind often; personalize them, visualize them. Keep them by your bedside and make them a morning prayer. Leave your small notebook open to these verses.

A few more verses to consider memorizing from Psalms:

Psalm 1:1-3; Psalm 9:10; Psalm 62:1-2; Psalm 139:13-14; Psalm 143:8

Lord,

As we reflect on and memorize Psalm 25:3–4, lead us to more treasures in the book of Psalms. Help us develop a new appreciation for the artistry of your Holy Spirit. We praise You for giving a voice to men who eloquently spoke of Your attributes and Your deep love and faithfulness. You filled them with your Spirit, which makes it possible for us to praise You now. May our voices mix with theirs until we meet again, to sing praises to You in Heaven together. In Jesus's name, Amen.

WEEK 5

NOON VERSE

"The will of God will never take you where the grace of God cannot keep you, where the arms of God cannot support you, where the riches of His grace cannot supply your needs."

~ Victor Knowles

PROVERBS 4:25–26

Let your eyes look straight ahead, fix your gaze directly before you. Make level paths for your feet and take only ways that are firm.

In 1 Kings 3:5, it says, "The Lord appeared to Solomon in a dream and said, 'Ask for whatever you want me to give you.'" Long story short, David's son Solomon asked for wisdom and discernment in leading God's people, and God gave him what he asked for and then some.

Spend time reading 1 Kings, chapters 1-11. You'll see a glimpse of all the treasures Solomon possessed. His story is carried on in 1 Chronicles as well. Both King David and his son, King Solomon were used mightily by God. He called David "a man after His own heart," and gave Solomon riches and wisdom beyond compare.

At some point, both men's power, importance, and lust sidetracked them. Yet, God worked through their failures, showing us that He can use anyone's life, messes and all, for His good purposes.

Just like these wise but flawed men, we strive for wisdom, but often realize we are foolish—our best intentions turn out badly. This is why the wisdom and warnings of Proverbs are still relevant today.

However, it's good to note that these proverbs are not commands to obey but more like fatherly advice to help us navigate our way through life—and stern warnings to steer us away from danger.

The book of Proverbs has thirty-one chapters. Many Christians read one chapter a day for a month. If you haven't done this yet or it's been a while, consider it as part of your quiet time for one month this year.

Place an X in the boxes when you've completed the Rs.

☐ READ

Read all of Proverbs 4 out loud. Notice the various admonitions. Note them here:

_____

_____

_____

_____

_____

PROVERBS 4:25–26

*Let your eyes look straight ahead, fix your gaze
directly before you. Make level paths for your feet
and take only ways that are firm.*

☐ REFLECT

Think about the effect these verses could have on your life. Do you always glance around and wonder what's going on? Do the paths you take end up in good places, or do you stumble too often, skin your knees, twist your ankle, or fall in a ditch? How long does it take you to get back on track? These verses can help us focus on what's straight in front of us, taking only the ways we know are right. Always seek God's wisdom in every circumstance you face. How could these verses help you in your daily walk with the Lord?

_____

_____

_____

_____

_____

_____

☐ RESTRUCTURE

Look at the verses and notice the progression—*always* ahead, *never* swerving side to side. Notice what it says about your eyes, your gaze, and then your feet. Notice the way the verse can be divided. Visualize what it would look like to walk this way. The verse has a repetition of words beginning with the letter *F*: fix, feet, firm. There is also an order to the verse's reference as well.

PROVERBS 4:25–26

*Let your eyes look straight ahead, fix your gaze
directly before you. Make level paths for your feet
and take only ways that are firm.*

Write down and rearrange the verse in a few different ways to help you think about
how to memorize it.

1. _____

_____

_____

2. _____

_____

_____

3. _____

_____

_____

When you see a pattern for the verse, memorize it that way. Write it down in
your spiral notebook.

☐ REHEARSE

Put this Scripture on repeat for the week. However, don't neglect the previous verse
from Psalms. Keep it close as well. Put this new one in other places—maybe where
you put your shoes on in the morning.

☐ REMEMBER

Try to write the verse without looking at it. Think about it as you make decisions and mull it over in your mind. Practice staying on solid ground, remembering this verse as you walk from place to place this week. Perhaps repeat it to someone you know.

☐ REVIEW

Add this verse to the one you already know from Psalms. Review them both.

A few more verses to consider memorizing from Proverbs:
Proverbs 3:5-6, Proverbs 12:18, Proverbs 18:10, Proverbs 27:1

God,

We long to walk in wisdom. We can only do that as we listen to Your voice and obey what You say. We've seen people fall by the wayside or veer off into places we know will cause trouble. We've done it ourselves. Lord, forgive us when we wander and set us back on the right road. Give us eyes to see what's in front of us and the strength to walk in a way that pleases You. May the gift of wisdom You gave Solomon help us in our daily lives. In Christ's name, amen.

NIGHT VERSE

"Real contentment must come from within. You and I cannot change or control the world around us, but we can change and control the world within us."

~ Warren Wiersbe

Philippians 4:8

Finally, brothers, whatever is true, whatever is noble, whatever is right, whatever is pure, whatever is lovely, whatever is admirable—if anything is excellent or praiseworthy—think about such things.

The New Testament contains twenty-seven books: the Gospels, Acts, the Epistles, and Revelation. The first four books, the Gospels, are accounts from men who either knew Jesus personally—Matthew and John—or interviewed eyewitnesses who did—Mark and Luke. Each one of them emphasized different aspects of Jesus's birth, life, death, and resurrection. The book of Acts relays amazing first-hand knowledge of what happened on earth after Jesus ascended to Heaven.

In addition to these books, we discover a treasure trove of personal letters. Thirteen of them are attributed to the Apostle Paul. After his miraculous encounter with Jesus on the road to Damascus, and a time of intense preparation, he went on four missionary journeys to spread the news of the risen Savior. His inspired letters were written mainly to churches he started and had continued contact with throughout his life. A few of them were written to his dear sons in the faith, Timothy and Titus, plus a dear friend, Philemon.

The Bible ends with the book of Revelation, which is stunning prophecy regarding the end times. Just as the Jewish nation struggled to understand the prophets, we struggle to understand John's book of Revelation. Many Bible scholars have dug deep into its meaning and message. A clear consensus has not been found. Although some prophecies are debated, and dates and times are questioned, one thing is clear: someday at the end of all things on earth and the beginning of all things in heaven, we will know the truth in full.

Although these books and letters are over two thousand years old, they speak to our hearts today. Many of Jesus's words and precious promises are gathered here for us to contemplate, learn, worship, and obey. However, not everything is prescribed for us in a literal sense. We do not chop our hands off or gouge our eyes out if they cause us to sin (Matthew 5:29–30). We will encounter problems if we try to follow everything in today's world. That's why it's important to understand hermeneutics; it's also vital to attend a Bible-believing church, and fellowship with other believers.

Place an X in the boxes when you've completed the Rs.

☐ READ

Read Paul's entire letter to the believers at Philippi. It's only four chapters long but is full of love, warmth, fatherly advice and admonition for believers who desire to grow in their faith. Pay close attention to 4:4–9. Although we are only going to learn one verse, I encourage you to memorize all of them. It's a wonderful passage on prayer and keeping our minds on praiseworthy things.

I struggled to memorize this particular verse in Philippians. As you come across certain passages of Scripture, you'll find that some of them are more challenging than others. This verse is one of them.

What are some verses that stand out to you in Paul's letter to the church in Philippi?

_____

_____

_____

_____

_____

_____

PHILIPPIANS 4: 8

Finally, brothers, whatever is true, whatever is noble, whatever is right, whatever is pure, whatever is lovely, whatever is admirable—if anything is excellent or praiseworthy—think about such things.

☐ REFLECT

How is your thought life? Do you thank God for each day and contemplate what's good and right? Where do your thoughts take you when you're done with your day? Look up some of the attributes in this verse for a better understanding and note your discoveries here:

_____

_____

_____

_____

_____

☐ RESTRUCTURE

Here's where memorizing the first letter of each word comes in handy. I made up the acronym TNRPLA, pronounced "Ten or Play" to help me visualize the key words in this verse: True, Noble, Right, Pure, Lovely, Admirable. Next, the *whatevers* give my mind a chance to ponder the next word, and the dashes after the list help me finish the verse. It makes sense to me. I hope it makes sense to you. Similar things will help *you* as you continue your memorization journey.

Write the verse down in a few different ways

1. _____

_____

_____

2. _____

_____

_____

3. _____

_____

_____

When you discover how you want to memorize it, write it in your Scripture notebook.

☐ REHEARSE

Among other places, be sure to put this verse beside your bed at night. It can be difficult to calm our thoughts when we try to sleep. We tend to rehearse the day and fret about things that went wrong. Instead, concentrate on what went right. Meditate on God's goodness as you go to sleep.

☐ REMEMBER

Write the verse out. Carry it in your pocket or put it in your phone. Look at it when you wait for a doctor, or pick kids up after school, or anywhere where a little free time is available. Say it in your mind, speak it out loud, or recite it to someone.

☐ REVIEW

Add this verse in Philippians to the verses from Psalms and Proverbs. Review all three until you know them well.

More verses from Philippians
Philippians 1:6, Philippians 2:1-2, Philippians 3:10, Philippians 4:4-8

Dear Lord,

Your Word is full of immense treasure for us to discover. Give us insight as we continue to meditate on and memorize Scripture. We want to understand Your Word and put it into practice. Thank you for providing ordinary men and women to tell stories of Your salvation and sanctification. We all have a story too. No one can take away our testimony, nor the words we memorize from the Bible. Sometimes we become discouraged with the pace of our spiritual progress, but You are always there to lift us back up. Your words have the power to forgive us, heal us, give us hope, and embrace the love and grace you freely offer. May we learn and grow as much as we can this side of heaven. In Christ's name, Amen.

PART THREE

NOW WHAT?

"For the word of God is living and active. Sharper than any double-edged sword, it penetrates even to dividing soul and spirit, joints and marrow; it judges the thoughts and attitudes of the heart."

~ Hebrews 4:12

Put Scripture into Practice

*W*hatever you do, don't close this book or put away your Scripture notebook. Stay invested! Boldly use what you learn as you read, reflect, rehearse, and remember God's Word. Stay close to Christ and put the truth into practice.

When we keep verses securely inside our hearts, we can commune with God anywhere at any time: in crowds, alone, as we pace in a waiting room or prepare for surgery, when we sit in a meeting, or when we're stuck in traffic or enclosed in an MRI machine. We don't always have access to our Bibles or our phones. And, if things go south in this crazy world, I want to be with people who know significant portions of Scripture. I also desire to be one of those people.

Consider how you might use the following verses in your life or share them with others? Read them out loud.

Spiritual Well-being

For the word of God is living and active. Sharper than any double-edged sword, it penetrates even to dividing soul and spirit, joints and marrow; it judges the thoughts and attitudes of the heart. (Hebrews 4:12)

The Truth

Do your best to present yourself to God as one approved, a workman who does not need to be ashamed and who correctly handles the word of truth. (2 Timothy 2:15)

A Renewed Mind

Do not conform any longer to the pattern of this world but be transformed by the renewing of your mind. Then you will be able to test and approve what God's will is—his good, pleasing and perfect will. (Romans 12:2)

Experience Healing

Therefore, confess your sins to each other and pray for each other, so that you may be healed. The prayer of a righteous man is powerful and effective. (James 5:16)

Evangelism

But in your hearts, set apart Christ as Lord. Always be prepared to give an answer to everyone who asks you to give the reason for the hope that you have. (1 Peter 3:15)

Helping Others

All Scripture is God-breathed and is useful for teaching, rebuking, correcting and training in righteousness, so that the man of God may be thoroughly equipped for every good work. (2 Timothy 3:16)

Effective Prayer Life

And pray in the Spirit on all occasions with all kinds of prayers and requests. With this in mind, be alert, and always keep on praying for all the saints. (Ephesians 6:18)

Filled with Love

I pray that you, being rooted and established in love, may have power, together with all the saints, to grasp how wide and long and high and deep is the love of Christ, and to know this love that surpasses knowledge—that you may be filled to the measure of all the fullness of God. (Ephesians 3:17–19)

Ready for Combat

Finally, be strong in the Lord and in his mighty power. Put on the full armor of God so that you can take your stand against the devil's schemes. (Ephesians 6:10–11)

Avoid Sin

I have hidden your word in my heart, that I might not sin against you. (Psalm 119:11)

Live with Hope

For everything that was written in the past was written to teach us, so that through endurance and the encouragement of the Scriptures, we might have hope. (Romans 15:4)

Walk in the Spirit

Those who belong to Christ Jesus have crucified the sinful nature with its passions and desires. Since we live by the Spirit, let us keep in step with the Spirit. (Galatians 5:24–25)

Consider the following stories. What Scriptural principles or passages come to mind? How would knowing Scripture help you minister to others?

Story #1: Compassion and Comfort

John called his sister, Diane, from the hospital. "Dad is sick, and the doctors don't think he's going to make it. I really could use some help here," he said.

Diane felt her stomach drop and knew this day was inevitable. "Okay, I'll get on the road as soon as I can."

She reluctantly traveled the seven hours to get to her father's side, fretting the whole way. Sue hadn't seen her dad in years. After her mom died, she decided to move away. Her dad had been abusive when she was young, and Sue didn't see any point in trying to have a relationship with him.

When she arrived, her brother filled her in on the medical details and then asked if he could leave for a while. He had been at the bedside most of the time and needed a break. He warned Diane that their dad woke up occasionally tried to talk. "It's not pleasant," he said.

How bad could it be? Diane had gotten used to her dad's demeaning remarks and sarcasm. She was never good enough—although her brother seemed to get along okay with him. Diane started to regret the decision she made, but after spending some time in prayer, she felt more at peace. The truth was, she was hoping to mend fences if she could. *Maybe things will be different this time.*

Two nurses soon came in to check on her dad and then moved him to a different position to alleviate soreness. He woke up, looked at Diane, and mumbled, "What are *you* doing here? Think I'm dying? Go home. I don't need you."

Diane swallowed hard and tears formed in her eyes. "John asked me to come," she said.

"Well, that's nice," he said with a tone she knew too well.

Her dad soon fell back to sleep, and she was glad. When John returned, she made a quick excuse to leave the room. She went to the cafeteria, got some coffee, then took a walk and ended up in the hospital chapel.

Why did I come here? I knew this would happen. Why would I expect anything different?

She heard a noise behind her and looked back to see the chaplain who had been in her dad's room that morning. They exchanged small talk, then the chaplain asked if she wanted company for a bit. She was taking a little break herself. Before long, Diane was pouring out the whole story, unable to stop the tears rolling down her face.

"What should I do? My brother wants me here, but I can't bear to go back in that room again."

Now change places with the chaplain. You are the one sitting there, listening to her. I learned early on in chaplain ministry that silence and prayer are invaluable, talking is not. Discerning a situation requires focused listening. When someone is going through an extremely difficult situation, they need words that help, not hurt.

What truth could you tell her from Scripture? How would you comfort her? Could this situation help her spiritually? What does she need? What could you pray for as you sit there with her?

A Better Way

Don't let your emotions get tangled up in the situation. (James 1:19–20)

Rejection and abuse are soul crushing. Take time to acknowledge the pain of her predicament. (1 Pet. 3:8)

God never leaves or abandons us. Even if our fathers, mothers, spouse, or children leave us, God will not. (Ps. 27:10)

She can accept the reality, grieve, forgive, and go on, knowing she will always be perfectly loved by God. (Eph. 4:15)

Pray with her for guidance. She will need to decide about her next step. Remember the decision is hers to make. (James 1:5)

Write your thoughts and insights here:

_____

_____

_____

_____

_____

_____

Story #2: Empty Empathy

Jeri knew she should call someone. But who? This diagnosis was life-threatening, and she was scared. Terrified, actually. The person who popped into her mind was her sister. Her husband had just gone through cancer treatments. She would understand.

Becky picked up on the third ring. "Hi, Jeri, what's going on?"

"I just got back from the doctor. He told me some bad news. I don't even want to say it out loud, but I need to let someone know. I have lung cancer."

Becky paused, then said, "I'm sorry. I knew you weren't looking well. When Sam got sick, I thought the worst. But now, I'm glad it's behind us. He didn't have a lot of side effects, so that was good."

"I don't know what the treatments will be yet," Jeri said. "I have an appointment with the oncologist set up."

"Did they say it was caused by smoking?"

"Well, I'm sure that didn't help, but I'm still glad I quit ten years ago. He didn't give a reason."

"Remember when Uncle Larry had lung cancer?" Becky asked. "Yikes! It was so hard on him. But maybe yours will go better. Whatever you need, you let us know. I can call the church prayer chain if you'd like."

"No thanks. I'll call the pastor and let him know. I gotta go now. Bye."

"Love you. Talk to you soon. Goodbye."

Spend some time identifying the problems with this scenario. If Jeri had chosen to call you instead, what would you have done? Would you take a deep breath and not make it about yourself? How would you approach the Holy Spirit for help? Could you remind her of God's love and provision? Would you assure her you'd be there for her? And then follow up? What would a prayer for her include?

A Better Way

Be compassionate and remember how God has helped you. (Phil 2:1)

Fear and anxiety fade when people are loved unconditionally. (1 John 4:18)

God will give her strength as she depends on Him. (2 Cor. 12:9)

Offer support and encouragement throughout the time of sickness. (Gal. 6:2)

Pray with her now and promise continued prayers. (Eph. 6:18)

Write your thoughts and insights here:

_____

_____

_____

_____

_____

Story #3: When the Truth Hurts

Sunlight filtered through the window. *Morning already!* Ann wondered if she had gotten any sleep. She suddenly remembered a snippet of a dream, so she assumed she had at least closed her eyes.

The uncertainty of the future loomed large ahead. *How am I going to get through this day?* Last night's fiasco came flooding in and she felt her chest tighten. *What if Ted finds out?*

As Ann got ready for work, she thought about who she could call for advice. She concluded that no one would understand how she got herself into this mess. A man she had known before she got married suddenly showed back up in her life. They ran across each other in a coffee shop and innocently sat down to catch up.

That was weeks ago. Then the texts and phone calls took place, and so the secrets began. Before long, they were meeting out of town, growing closer emotionally. The flirtatious fling soon turned into more than she could handle.

She discovered this man, who she remembered fondly from high school, had a drinking problem. He wanted Ann to go farther physically. When she refused, he didn't stop trying. He got aggressive, swore at her, then told her to get out of the car. He left her there on the side of the road.

Ann made it home and took a long shower, trying to wash away what had happened. Ted was out of town on business but would be back tomorrow. *How can I pretend nothing happened?*

If Ann decides to call you, what do you think she needs? Would you help her without judging her? Could you lovingly confront her? What would you encourage her to do? Could you have compassion for her?

Life is treacherous at times, and we get ourselves into messes that are hard to get out of. We go down a road we know is wrong yet minimize our reasons for taking it. Finding our way back, we try to bypass the pain, but it never works. What do we need during those times when we blow it?

A Better Way

Know it could happen to you too. We all fall short. (1 Cor. 10:13)

Acknowledge the truth of the sin and the remedy. (1 John 1:9)

Encourage telling the truth about what she's done. (Heb. 4:13)

Reassurance of God's ability to cause all things to work for good. (Rom. 8:28)

Write your thoughts and insights here:

_____

_____

_____

_____

_____

_____

_____

A Real-Life Reflection

Sometimes we lose someone, and it shatters us. Our heart splinters into a million pieces and we're never the same. We relive the details of the death, on repeat, explicitly, excruciatingly, for a long time. This most often happens when there's a tragic accident, a murder, a suicide, or the sudden death of a young child. Things don't go in the right order. Your loved ones are supposed to be born, live a long life, and then pass away peacefully in their sleep.

My granddaughter, Dylan, has been gone for eight years now. She was my only daughter's only daughter. She died suddenly when she was ten years old after a lifetime of being in and out of hospitals. My granddaughter was perfectly fine, except for the arteriovenous malformation in her brain, which required several surgeries and procedures. During her short life, she had many ups and downs—and plenty of heartbreaking setbacks. However, Dylan was a beautiful, funny, creative, and loving person. She loved Jesus—and she knew Jesus loved her.

I miss her every day, but I know that Dylan is with Jesus, perfect and happy and free from sorrow. We know from God's Word that we will see her again.

Since taking this eight-year grief journey with my daughter, Melissa, some of the support she and her husband receive is wonderful, but sometimes things are said that are both painful and annoying.

You have an angel watching over you
God needed her more
It was her time
She got her wings
She's in a better place

These are statements—a way of explaining away the devastation of Dylan's death. Sometimes people want to tie grief up in a pretty bow, hoping it will lessen the pain. It doesn't.

You can't convince people it will be okay or take away their grief or come up with reasons why it happened. Unless you are extremely close to the person and know them well, the less you say the better. The more you *do* the better.

Bear the burden with them. Show compassion. (Gal. 6:2)
If one in the Body suffers, we all suffer. (1 Cor. 12:25)
Don't make it about yourself; be humble. (Phil. 2-3)
If you can provide something, provide it. (Proverbs 3:27)
Be sensitive to the Holy Spirit (Gal. 5:16)

For these stories and many like them, we need to do our best to stay clean and close with God, walking in obedience and abiding in His grace. Even if we blow it sometimes (and we will) God's grace is bigger than our goof-ups. If we say something wrong or hurtful to someone, we can apologize. If that's not possible, we can learn from the experience and do our best not to repeat it.

I recall times I've blown it and have experienced others falter as well. I've known pastors to give bad council, good friends who were insensitive, family members who judge and random Christians who slander or gossip without knowing any details. That's why we need a Savior who convicts us of our sin, forgives us, and encourages us to grow and become more like Him.

Spend time in the Bible, seek God's truth, embrace His love for you, memorize His Word, and let the Holy Spirit put it into practice in your life.

> *"Do your best to present yourself as one approved, a workman who*
> *doesn't need to be ashamed but correctly handles the truth."*
> *~ 2 Tim. 2:15*

Lord,

Enable us to love those around us, both family, friends, enemies and strangers. Remind us often that you died for every one of us and it's only by your grace we are saved. Give us compassion to look past the person into the soul. We're here because you created each one of us. Give us humility and grace as we interact with our fellow man. Show us, teach us, guide us in Your truth. We long to trust You—morning, noon and night. In Your Son's name we pray, amen.

GOALS FOR THE NEXT SIX MONTHS

_____ through _____, 20____

I _____ commit to the following activities as a spiritual discipline to grow closer to God and to be a blessing to those God brings in my path; I will continue to pursue accountability with a friend, spouse, group, or online.

- Memorize additional verses in Psalms, Proverbs and Philippians.
- Review all your verses weekly.
- Fill up your fifty-page Scripture notebook with verses to work on.
- Memorize a longer passage: start with the following verses from Romans:

O, the depths of the riches of the wisdom and knowledge of God! How unsearchable his judgments and his paths beyond tracing out! Who has known the mind of the Lord? Or who has been his counselor? Who has ever given to God that God should repay him? For from him and through him and to him are all things. To him be the glory forever. Amen.

Therefore, I urge you, brothers, in view of God's mercy, offer your bodies as living sacrifices, holy and pleasing to God—this is your spiritual act of worship. Do not conform any longer to the pattern of this world but be transformed by the renewing of your mind. Then, you will be able to test and approve what God's will is—his good, pleasing, and perfect will.

~ Romans 11:33–12:6

A Blessing

May the Lord open your eyes to clearly see His Word; may He give you a deep desire to memorize Scripture and empower you to use what you learn. May He comfort you with His love and heal anything in you that is bruised, crushed, or broken. May you always sense His presence no matter where you are or what you face, and may you let Him use you to mightily minister to others.

Marla

God can't give us happiness and peace apart from Himself
because there is no such thing.
~ C.S.Lewis

ACKNOWLEDGMENTS

The process of writing your first book and having it published is no small task. I'm grateful I had the publishing team of Illumify Media's help along the way. I would highly recommend the hybrid route for first-time authors.

Michael Klassen, your expertise in all areas of writing and publishing is an inspiration to me. I'm thankful for all you do for aspiring authors, bringing their books to life. Your Power Writer's Report is something I look forward to reading weekly—and I always come away encouraged. Thank you, especially for your continued support throughout this adventure.

Jennifer Clark, you make complicated things simpler. Your down-to-earth style is refreshing. Thanks for helping me navigate through the process of publishing and working with me in the details. As I write this, our work is not finished, but I'm confident we will see it through.

And, Geoffrey Stone, your editing skills are a gift! Much of writing a book is about rewriting. Thanks for helping me find better ways of saying what I wanted to say. Your patience with repeated copy edits was appreciated.

Debbie Lewis, thanks for your time and attention to creating the book cover that I had in mind.

Also, to Kara Acino, Marti Wibbels, and Melissa Tolen, thank you for walking beside me. You each contributed unique insights, timely encouragement, and much needed prayer.

RESOURCES

10 Mnemonics that Help You Remember Anything, https://www.verywellhealth.com/memory-tip-1-keyword-mnemonics-98466

    Bibledictionary.com

    Biblegateway.com

    BibleMemory.com

    BibleMemoryGoal.com

    Biblestudytools.com

    Discipleship.org

    Dwell.com

    Navigators.org

A Few More Verses to Consider for Your First Fifty

Have I not commanded you? Be strong and courageous. Do not be terrified and do not be discouraged, for the Lord your God will be with you wherever you go. (Joshua 1:9)

May the words of my mouth and the meditation of my heart be pleasing in your sight, O Lord, my Rock and my Redeemer. (Psalm 19:14)

Therefore, do not worry about tomorrow, for tomorrow will worry about itself. Each day has enough trouble of its own. (Matthew 6:34)

Pray in the Spirit on all occasions with all kinds of prayers and requests. With this in mind, be alert, and always keep on praying for all the saints. (Ephesians 6:18)

For God has not given us a spirit of timidity, but a spirit of power, of love and of self-discipline. (2 Timothy 1:7)

Consider Him who endured such opposition from sinful men, so that you will not grow weary and lose heart. (Hebrews 12:3)

Dear children, let us not love with words or tongue but with actions and in truth. (1 John 3:18)

ABOUT THE AUTHOR

*M*arla Kohmetscher is a retired hospital chaplain from Grand Island, Nebraska, and former director of a crisis pregnancy center. She has a bachelor's degree in Christian ministry and minor in biblical studies from Grace University. Marla has a lifetime love of memorizing Scripture and understands the importance of using God's Word wisely in real life situations.

Marla has also been involved in women's ministry leadership, facilitated numerous Bible studies, and led weekend retreats for women called Seasons of Change.

She enjoys spending time outside in her flower garden, and when the weather isn't cooperating, she sews one-of-a-kind quilts and dabbles in other creative endeavors. Marla has three children, six grandchildren on earth, and three in heaven. She also has two great-grandchildren. She can be found at marlakohmetscher.com.